DATE DUE

APR 0 5 2006	
APR 2 6 2006	
GAYLORD	PRINTED IN U.S.A.

Roald Dahl
Vile Verses

Roald Dahl

VILE VERSES

Viking

VIKING
Published by Penguin Group
Penguin Young Readers Group, 345 Hudson Street, New York, New York 10014, U.S.A.

Penguin Books Ltd, Registered Offices: 80 Strand, London WC2R 0RL, England

First published in Great Britain in 2005 by Jonathan Cape, an imprint of Random House Children's Books.

Published in the United States in 2005 by Viking, a division of Penguin Young Readers Group

Contents

FOREWORD

Part One

THERE ARE THINGS TO SEE AND DO

Part Two

BEST BEHAVIOUR

Part Six

ALL TOGETHER NOW

Part Seven

AND A FEW SURPRISES

INDEX

Foreword

It's hard to read one of your favourite Dahl books without soon coming across some kind of song or a piece of verse. I can remember when I first read *The Enormous Crocodile*, before I did the pictures for it; no sooner has the Croc started talking about eating some juicy little children for lunch than he makes a verse about it: "I'm going to fill my hungry empty tummy/With something yummy yummy yummy yummy!"

There are poems in the longer books too – in *The Witches*, in *Charlie and the Chocolate Factory*, and *James and the Giant Peach*. If you start to count up all these moments you discover that there are really quite a lot of them; and in fact this is just what someone at Roald Dahl's publishers did, some time ago, and suggested that it would be a good idea to bring as many of them as possible to one book.

That is the book that you have in your hands now. In putting it together we realized that we could include extra poems, such as one that Roald Dahl left out of *Charlie* because he found that he had invented just too many dreadful children. It was also hard not to include some of the favourites from those Dahl books which are exclusively of verse, like *Revolting Rhymes* or *Dirty Beasts*.

Once the poems were arranged into sections there came the question, how should they be illustrated? The answer, as far as I am concerned, has made this book particularly interesting and exciting.

At the present time most of the Dahl books in the shops have pictures which I drew specially for them; and many of them which I had discussed with Roald Dahl himself. But there are several Dahl books which have been previously illustrated – and very well illustrated – by other people, and it's interesting to compare different versions. So we thought – what about getting a whole assortment of talented artists to join in on the book, and see what their interpretations of Dahl are like?

We've been all over the world for our artists and there is a wonderful assortment here from the well-established to young illustrators who, if not already stars, are shining more brightly day by day.

For me, there are two special areas of interest in all the diverse pictures they have produced. One is that there are some poems that have previously never been illustrated – like the Centipede's song from *James*. If you are illustrating the book you can draw the Centipede waving his many boots and singing; but you can't really ask for two or three extra pages to show *all* the bizarre things that are mentioned. Now we get a chance to have a proper look at it.

The other is where poems that have been illustrated before are illustrated again in a new way – it reminds me of being present at another production of a Shakespeare play or the performance of a piece of music and saying to yourself, yes, that's another way of doing it and that's right as well.

While all this was going on they said to me that I didn't have to work too hard and I could be a sort of presenter. So I have done the cover, and some drawings for the openings of the sections. We've had a really good time putting this book together; we hope you get even more enjoyment from reading it and looking at it. Welcome once again to the world of Roald Dahl.

Quentin Blake

Part One

THERE ARE THINGS TO SEE AND DO

The Giraffe and the Pelly and Me

from THE GIRAFFE AND THE PELLY AND ME
Illustrated by Chris Wormell

We will polish your glass
Till it's shining like brass
And it sparkles like sun on the sea!
We are quick and polite,
We will come day or night,
The Giraffe and the Pelly and me!

We're a fabulous crew,
We know just what to do,
And we never stop work to drink tea.
All your windows will glow
When we give them a go,
The Giraffe and the Pelly and me!

We use water and soap
Plus some kindness and hope,
But we never use ladders, not we.
Who needs ladders at all
When you're thirty feet tall?
Not Giraffe, and not Pelly! Not me!

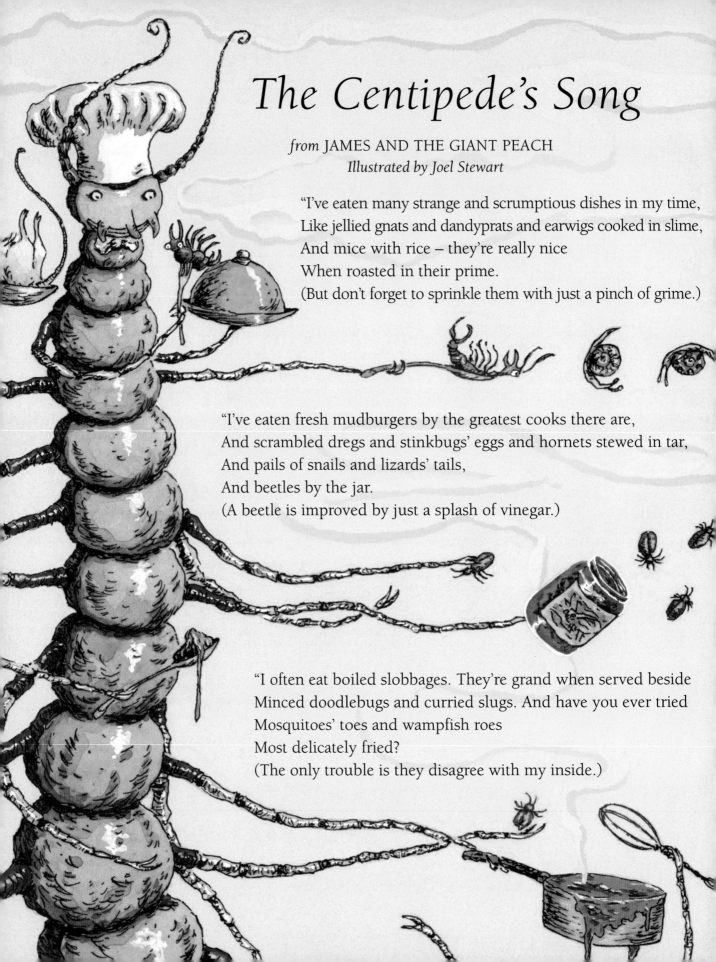

The Centipede's Song

from JAMES AND THE GIANT PEACH
Illustrated by Joel Stewart

"I've eaten many strange and scrumptious dishes in my time,
Like jellied gnats and dandyprats and earwigs cooked in slime,
And mice with rice – they're really nice
When roasted in their prime.
(But don't forget to sprinkle them with just a pinch of grime.)

"I've eaten fresh mudburgers by the greatest cooks there are,
And scrambled dregs and stinkbugs' eggs and hornets stewed in tar,
And pails of snails and lizards' tails,
And beetles by the jar.
(A beetle is improved by just a splash of vinegar.)

"I often eat boiled slobbages. They're grand when served beside
Minced doodlebugs and curried slugs. And have you ever tried
Mosquitoes' toes and wampfish roes
Most delicately fried?
(The only trouble is they disagree with my inside.)

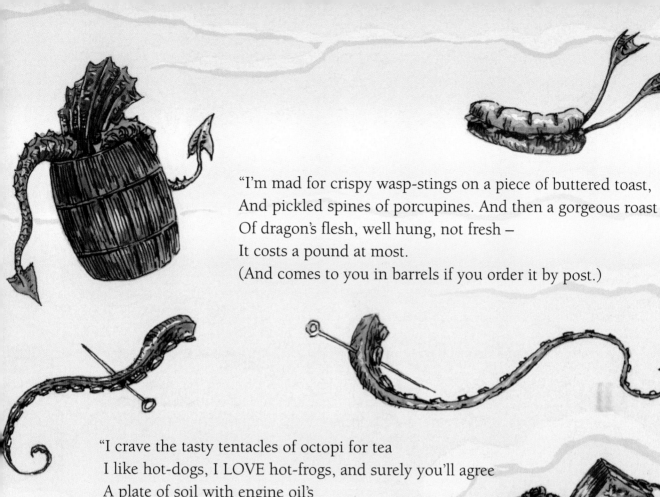

"I'm mad for crispy wasp-stings on a piece of buttered toast,
And pickled spines of porcupines. And then a gorgeous roast
Of dragon's flesh, well hung, not fresh –
It costs a pound at most.
(And comes to you in barrels if you order it by post.)

"I crave the tasty tentacles of octopi for tea
I like hot-dogs, I LOVE hot-frogs, and surely you'll agree
A plate of soil with engine oil's
A super recipe.
(I hardly need to mention that it's practically free.)

"For dinner on my birthday shall I tell you what I chose:
Hot noodles made from poodles on a slice of garden hose –
And a rather smelly jelly
Made of armadillo's toes.
(The jelly is delicious, but you have to hold your nose.)

"Now comes," the Centipede declared, "the burden of my speech:
These foods are rare beyond compare – some are right out of reach;
But there's no doubt I'd go without
A million plates of each
For one small mite,
One tiny bite,
Of this FANTASTIC PEACH!"

Another Centipede Song

from JAMES AND THE GIANT PEACH
Illustrated by Chris Riddell

"Oh, hooray for the storm and the rain!
I can move! I don't feel any pain!
And now I'm a pest,
I'm the biggest and best,
The most marvellous pest once again!"

"Oh, do shut up," the Old-Green-Grasshopper said.
"Look at me!" cried the Centipede.

"Look at ME! I am freed! I am freed!
Not a scratch nor a bruise nor a bleed!
To his grave this fine gent
They all thought they had sent
And I very near went!
Oh, I VERY near went!
But they cent quite the wrong Sentipede!"

Willy Wonka's Wonka-Vite

from CHARLIE AND THE GREAT GLASS ELEVATOR
Illustrated by Geefwee Boedoe

Come on, old friends, and do what's right!
Come make your lives as bright as bright!
Just take a dose of this delight!
This heavenly magic dynamite!
You can't go wrong, you must go right!
IT'S WILLY WONKA'S WONKA-VITE!
If you are old and have the shakes,
If all your bones are full of aches,
If you can hardly walk at all,
If living drives you up the wall,
If you're a grump and full of spite,
If you're a human parasite,
THEN WHAT YOU NEED IS WONKA-VITE!
Your eyes will shine, your hair will grow,
Your face and skin will start to glow,
Your rotten teeth will all drop out
And in their place new teeth will sprout.

Those rolls of fat around your hips
Will vanish, and your wrinkled lips
Will get so soft and rosy-pink
That all the boys will smile and wink
And whisper secretly that this
Is just the girl they want to kiss!
But wait! For that is not the most
Important thing of which to boast.
Good looks you'll have, we've told you so,
But looks aren't everything, you know.
Each pill, as well, to you will give
AN EXTRA TWENTY YEARS TO LIVE!
So come, old friends, and do what's right!
Let's make your lives as bright as bright!
Let's take a dose of this delight!
This heavenly magic dynamite!
You can't go wrong, you must go right!
IT'S WILLY WONKA'S WONKA-VITE!

Part Two

BEST
BEHAVIOUR

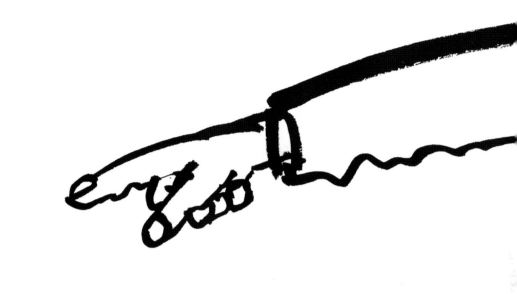

Snow-White and the Seven Dwarfs

from REVOLTING RHYMES
Illustrated by Babette Cole

When little Snow-White's mother died,
The king, her father, up and cried,
"Oh, what a nuisance! What a life!
Now I must find another wife!"
(It's never easy for a king
To find himself that sort of thing.)
He wrote to every magazine
And said, "I'm looking for a Queen."

At least ten thousand girls replied
And begged to be the royal bride.
The king said with a shifty smile,
"I'd like to give each one a trial."

However, in the end he chose
A lady called Miss Maclahose,
Who brought along a curious toy
That seemed to give her endless joy –
This was a mirror framed in brass,
A MAGIC TALKING LOOKING-GLASS.
Ask it something day or night,
It always got the answer right.
For instance, if you were to say,
"Oh Mirror, what's for lunch today?"
The thing would answer in a trice,
"Today it's scrambled eggs and rice."
Now every day, week in week out,
The spoiled and stupid Queen would shout,
"Oh Mirror Mirror on the wall,
Who is the fairest of them all?"
The Mirror answered every time,
"Oh Madam, you're the Queen sublime.
You are the only one to charm us,
Queen, you are the cat's pyjamas."
For ten whole years the silly Queen
Repeated this absurd routine.
Then suddenly, one awful day,
She heard the Magic Mirror say,
"From now on, Queen, you're *Number Two*.
Snow-White is prettier than you!"

The Queen went absolutely wild.
She yelled, "I'm going to scrag that child!
I'll cook her flaming goose! I'll skin 'er!
I'll have her rotten guts for dinner!"
She called the Huntsman to her study.
She shouted at him, "Listen buddy!
You drag that filthy girl outside,
And see you take her for a ride!
Thereafter slit her ribs apart
And bring me back her bleeding heart!"

The Huntsman dragged the lovely child
Deep deep into the forest wild.
Fearing the worst, poor Snow-White spake.
She cried, "Oh please give me a break!"
The knife was poised, the arm was strong,
She cried again, "I've done no *wrong*!"
The Huntsman's heart began to flutter.
It melted like a pound of butter.
He murmured, "Okay, beat it, kid",
And you can bet your life she did.

Later, the Huntsman made a stop
Within the local butcher's shop,
And there he bought, for safety's sake,
A bullock's heart and one nice steak.
"Oh Majesty! Oh Queen!" he cried,
"That rotten little girl has died!
And just to prove I didn't cheat,
I've brought along these bits of meat."
The Queen cried out, "Bravissimo!
I trust you killed her nice and slow."
Then (this is the disgusting part)
The Queen sat down and ate the heart!
(I only hope she cooked it well.
Boiled heart can be as tough as hell.)

While all of this was going on,
Oh where, oh where had Snow-White gone?
She'd found it easy, being pretty,
To hitch a ride in to the city,
And there she'd got a job, unpaid,
As general cook and parlour-maid
With seven funny little men,
Each one not more than three foot ten,
Ex horse-race jockeys, all of them.
These Seven Dwarfs, though awfully nice,
Were guilty of one shocking vice –
They squandered all of their resources
At the race-track backing horses.
(When they hadn't backed a winner,
None of them got any dinner.)
One evening, Snow-White said, "Look here,
I think I've got a great idea.
Just leave it all to me, okay?
And no more gambling till I say."

That very night, at eventide,
Young Snow-White hitched another ride,
And then, when it was very late,
She slipped in through the Palace gate.
The King was in his counting house
Counting out his money,
The Queen was in the parlour
Eating bread and honey,
The footmen and the servants slept
So no one saw her as she crept
On tip-toe through the mighty hall
And grabbed THE MIRROR off the wall.

As soon as she had got it home,
She told the Senior Dwarf (or Gnome)
To ask it what he wished to know.
"Go on!" she shouted. "Have a go!"

He said, "Oh Mirror, please don't joke!
Each one of us is stony broke!
Which horse will win tomorrow's race,
The Ascot Gold Cup Steeplechase?"
The Mirror whispered sweet and low,
"The horse's name is Mistletoe."
The Dwarfs went absolutely daft,
They kissed young Snow-White fore and aft,
Then rushed away to raise some dough
With which to back old Mistletoe.

They pawned their watches, sold the car,
They borrowed money near and far,
(For much of it they had to thank
The manager of Barclays Bank.)
They went to Ascot and of course
For once they backed the winning horse.
Thereafter, every single day,
The Mirror made the bookies pay.
Each Dwarf and Snow-White got a share,
And each was soon a millionaire,
Which shows that gambling's not a sin
Provided that you always win.

Goldilocks and the Three Bears

from REVOLTING RHYMES
Illustrated by Lauren Child

This famous wicked little tale
Should never have been put on sale.
It is a mystery to me
Why loving parents cannot see
That this is actually a book
About a brazen little crook.
Had I the chance I wouldn't fail
To clap young Goldilocks in jail.
Now just imagine how *you'd* feel
If you had cooked a lovely meal,
Delicious porridge, steaming hot,
Fresh coffee in the coffee-pot,
With maybe toast and marmalade,
The table beautifully laid,
One place for you and one for dad,
Another for your little lad.
Then dad cries, "Golly-gosh! Gee-whizz!
Oh cripes! How hot this porridge is!
Let's take a walk along the street
Until it's cool enough to eat."
He adds, "An early morning stroll
Is good for people on the whole.
It makes your appetite improve
It also helps your bowels to move."
No proper wife would dare to question
Such a sensible suggestion,

Above all not at breakfast-time
When men are seldom at their prime.
No sooner are you down the road
Than Goldilocks, that little toad
That nosy thieving little louse
Comes sneaking in your empty house.
She looks around. She quickly notes
Three bowls brimful of porridge-oats.
And while still standing on her feet,
She grabs a spoon and starts to eat.
I say again, how *would* you feel
If you had made this lovely meal
And some delinquent little tot
Broke in and gobbled up the lot?
But wait! That's not the worst of it!
Now comes the most distressing bit.
You are of course a houseproud wife,
And all your happy married life
You have collected lovely things
Like gilded cherubs wearing wings,
And furniture by Chippendale
Bought at some famous auction sale.
But your most special valued treasure,
The piece that gives you endless pleasure,
Is one small children's dining-chair,
Elizabethan, very rare.
It is in fact your joy and pride,
Passed down to you on grandma's side.
But Goldilocks, like many freaks,
Does not appreciate antiques.
She doesn't care, she doesn't mind,
And now she plonks her fat behind
Upon this dainty precious chair,
And crunch! It busts beyond repair.

A nice girl would at once exclaim,
"Oh dear! Oh heavens! What a shame!"
Not Goldy. She begins to swear.
She bellows, "What a lousy chair!"
And uses *one* disgusting word
That luckily you've never heard.
(I dare not write it, even hint it.
Nobody would ever print it.)
You'd think by now this little skunk
Would have the sense to do a bunk.
But no. I very much regret
She hasn't nearly finished yet.
Deciding she would like a rest,
She says, "Let's see which bed is best."
Upstairs she goes and tries all three.
(Here comes the next catastrophe.)
Most educated people choose
To rid themselves of socks and shoes
Before they clamber into bed.
But Goldie didn't give a shred.
Her filthy shoes were thick with grime,
And mud and mush and slush and slime.
Worse still, upon the heel of one
Was something that a dog had done.
I say once more, what *would* you think
If all this horrid dirt and stink
Was smeared upon your eiderdown
By this revolting little clown?
(The famous story has no clues
To show the girl removed her shoes.)
Oh, what a tale of crime on crime!
Let's check it for a second time.

CRIME ONE:
The prosecution's case:
She breaks and enters someone's place.

CRIME TWO:
The prosecutor notes:
She steals a bowl of porridge oats.

CRIME THREE:
She breaks a precious chair
Belonging to the Baby Bear.

CRIME FOUR:
She smears each spotless sheet
With filthy messes from her feet.

A judge would say without a blink,
"Ten years' hard labour in the clink!"
But in the book, as you will see,
The little beast gets off scot-free,
While tiny children near and far
Shout, "Goody-good! Hooray! Hurrah!
Poor darling Goldilocks!" they say.
Thank goodness that she got away!"
Myself, I think I'd rather send
Young Goldie to a sticky end.
"Oh daddy!" cried the Baby Bear,
"My porridge gone! It isn't fair!"
"Then go upstairs," the Big Bear said,
"Your porridge is upon the bed.
But as it's inside mademoiselle,
You'll have to eat *her* up as well."

Concerning Augustus Gloop

from CHARLIE AND THE CHOCOLATE FACTORY
Illustrated by Mini Grey

Augustus Gloop! Augustus Gloop!
The great big greedy nincompoop!
How long could we allow this beast
To gorge and guzzle, feed and feast
On everything he wanted to?
Great Scott! It simply wouldn't do!
However long this pig might live,
We're positive he'd never give
Even the smallest bit of fun
Or happiness to anyone.
So what we do in cases such
As this, we use the gentle touch,
And carefully we take the brat
And turn him into something that
Will give great pleasure to us all –
A doll, for instance, or a ball,
Or marbles or a rocking horse.
But this revolting boy, of course,
Was so unutterably vile,
So greedy, foul, and infantile,
He left a most disgusting taste
Inside our mouths, and so in haste
We chose a thing that, come what may,
Would take the nasty taste away.

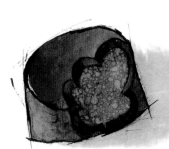

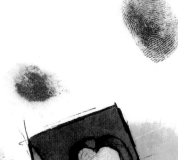

"Come on!" we cried. "The time is ripe
To send him shooting up the pipe!
He has to go! It has to be!"
And very soon, he's going to see
Inside the room to which he's gone
Some funny things are going on.
But don't, dear children, be alarmed;
Augustus Gloop will not be harmed,
Although, of course, we must admit
He will be altered quite a bit.

He'll be *quite* changed from what he's been,
When he goes through the fudge machine:
Slowly, the wheels go round and round,
The cogs begin to grind and pound;
A hundred knives go slice, slice, slice;
We add some sugar, cream and spice;
We boil him for a minute more,
Until we're absolutely sure
That all the greed and all the gall
Is boiled away for once and all.
Then out he comes! And now! By grace!
A miracle has taken place!
This boy, who only just before
Was loathed by men from shore to shore,
This greedy brute, this louse's ear,
Is loved by people everywhere!
For who could hate or bear a grudge
Against a luscious bit of fudge?

Concerning Mike Teavee

from CHARLIE AND THE CHOCOLATE FACTORY
Illustrated by Posy Simmonds

The most important thing we've learned,
So far as children are concerned,
Is never, NEVER, NEVER let
Them near your television set –
Or better still, just don't install
The idiotic thing at all.
In almost every house we've been,
We've watched them gaping at the screen.
They loll and slop and lounge about,
And stare until their eyes pop out.
(Last week in someone's place we saw
A dozen eyeballs on the floor.)
They sit and stare and stare and sit
Until they're hypnotized by it,
Until they're absolutely drunk
With all that shocking ghastly junk.
Oh yes, we know it keeps them still,
They don't climb out the window sill,
They never fight or kick or punch,
They leave you free to cook the lunch

And wash the dishes in the sink –
But did you ever stop to think,
To wonder just exactly what
This does to your beloved tot?
IT ROTS THE SENSES IN THE HEAD!
IT KILLS IMAGINATION DEAD!
IT CLOGS AND CLUTTERS UP THE MIND!
IT MAKES A CHILD SO DULL AND BLIND
HE CAN NO LONGER UNDERSTAND
A FANTASY, A FAIRYLAND!
HIS BRAIN BECOMES AS SOFT AS CHEESE!
HIS POWERS OF THINKING RUST AND FREEZE!
HE *CANNOT* THINK – HE ONLY SEES!
"All right!" you'll cry. "All right!" you'll say,
"But if we take the set away,
What shall we do to entertain
Our darling children! Please explain!"
We'll answer this by asking you,
"What used the darling ones to do?
How *used* they keep themselves contented
Before this monster was invented?"
Have you forgotten? Don't you know?
We'll say it very loud and slow:
THEY . . . USED . . . TO . . . READ! They'd READ and READ,
AND READ and READ, and then proceed
TO READ some more. Great Scott! Gadzooks!
One half their lives was reading books!
The nursery shelves held books galore!
Books cluttered up the nursery floor!
And in the bedroom, by the bed,
More books were waiting to be read!

Such wondrous, fine,
  fantastic tales
Of dragons, gypsies,
  queens, and whales

And treasure isles,
  and distant shores
Where smugglers rowed
  with muffled oars,

And pirates wearing
  purple pants,
And sailing ships
  and elephants,

And cannibals crouching
  round the pot,
Stirring away at something hot.
  (It smells so good, what can it be?
Good gracious, it's Penelope.)

The younger ones had Beatrix Potter
With Mr Tod, the dirty rotter,

And Squirrel Nutkin,
  Pigling Bland,
And Mrs Tiggy-Winkle and –

Just How The Camel
  Got His Hump,
And How The Monkey
  Lost His Rump,

And Mr Toad,
  and bless my soul,
There's Mr Rat and Mr Mole –

Oh, books, what books they used to know,
Those children living long ago!

So please, oh *please*, we beg, we pray,
Go throw your TV set away,
And in its place you can install
A lovely bookshelf on the wall.
Then fill the shelves with lots of books,
Ignoring all the dirty looks,
The screams and yells, the bites and kicks,
And children hitting you with sticks –
Fear not, because we promise you
That, in about a week or two
Of having nothing else to do,
They'll now begin to feel the need
Of having something good to read.
And once they start – oh boy, oh boy!
You watch the slowly growing joy
That fills their hearts. They'll grow so keen
They'll wonder what they'd ever seen
In that ridiculous machine,
That nauseating, foul, unclean,
Repulsive television screen!
And later, each and every kid
Will love you more for what you did.
P.S. Regarding Mike Teavee,
We very much regret that we
Shall simply have to wait and see
If we can get him back his height.
But if we can't – it serves him right.

Concerning Violet Beauregarde

from CHARLIE AND THE CHOCOLATE FACTORY
Illustrated by Mini Grey

Dear friends, we surely all agree
There's almost nothing worse to see
Than some repulsive little bum
Who's always chewing chewing-gum.
(It's very near as bad as those
Who sit around and pick the nose.)
So please believe us when we say
That chewing gum will never pay;
This sticky habit's bound to send
The chewer to a sticky end.
Did any of you ever know
A person called Miss Bigelow?
This dreadful woman saw no wrong
In chewing, chewing all day long.
She chewed while bathing in the tub,
She chewed while dancing at her club,
She chewed in church and on the bus;
It really was quite ludicrous!
And when she couldn't find her gum,
She'd chew up the linoleum,
Or anything that happened near –
A pair of boots, the postman's ear,
Or other people's underclothes,
And once she chewed her boyfriend's nose.

She went on chewing till, at last,
Her chewing muscles grew so vast
That from her face her giant chin
Stuck out just like a violin.
For years and years she chewed away,
Consuming fifty bits a day,
Until one summer's eve, alas,
A horrid business came to pass.
Miss Bigelow went late to bed,
For half an hour she lay and read,
Chewing and chewing all the while
Like some great clockwork crocodile.
At last, she put her gum away
Upon a special little tray,
And settled back and went to sleep –
(She managed this by counting sheep).
But now, how strange! Although she slept,
Those massive jaws of hers still kept
On chewing, chewing through the night,
Even with nothing there to bite.
They were, you see, in such a groove
They positively *had* to move.
And very grim it was to hear
In pitchy darkness, loud and clear,
This sleeping woman's great big trap
Opening and shutting, *snap-snap-snap*!
Faster and faster, *chop-chop-chop*,
The noise went on, it wouldn't stop.
Until at last her jaws decide
To pause and open extra wide,
And with the most tremendous chew
They bit the lady's tongue in two.

Thereafter, just from chewing gum,
Miss Bigelow was always dumb,
And spent her life shut up in some
Disgusting sanatorium.
And *that* is why we'll try so hard
To save Miss Violet Beauregarde
From suffering an equal fate.
She's still quite young. It's not too late,
Provided she survives the cure.
We hope she does. We can't be sure.

Concerning Veruca Salt

from CHARLIE AND THE CHOCOLATE FACTORY
Illustrated by Posy Simmonds

Veruca Salt, the little brute,
Has just gone down the rubbish chute
(And as we very rightly thought
That in a case like this we ought
To see the thing completely through,
We've polished off her parents, too).
Down goes Veruca! Down the drain!
And here, perhaps, we should explain
That she will meet, as she descends,
A rather different set of friends
To those that she has left behind –
These won't be nearly so refined.
A fish head, for example, cut
This morning from a halibut.
"Hello! Good morning! How d'you do?
How nice to meet you!
    How are you?"
And then a little further down
A mass of others gather round:
A bacon rind,
    some rancid lard,
A loaf of bread
    gone stale and hard,
A steak that nobody
    could chew,
An oyster from
an oyster stew,

Some liverwurst
  so old and grey
One smelled it from
  a mile away,
A rotten nut,
  a reeky pear,
A thing the cat
  left on the stair,
And lots of other things
  as well,
Each with a rather horrid smell.
These are Veruca's
  new-found friends
That she will meet as she descends,
And *this* is the price she has to pay
  For going so very far astray.
But now, my dears, we think you might
  Be wondering – is it really right
  That every single bit of blame
  And all the scolding and the shame
  Should fall upon Veruca Salt?
  Is *she* the only one at fault?
For though she's spoiled, and dreadfully so,
  A girl can't spoil herself, you know.
Who spoiled her, then? Ah, who indeed?
  Who pandered to her every need?
  Who turned her into such a brat?
  Who are the culprits? *Who* did that?
  Alas! You needn't look so far
  To find out who these sinners are.
  They are (and this is very sad)
Her loving parents, MUM and DAD.
  And that is why we're glad they fell
  Into the rubbish chute as well.

The Tortoise and the Hare

from RHYME STEW
Illustrated by Axel Scheffler

The Tortoise long ago had learned
(So far as eating was concerned)
That nothing in the world could match
Old Mister Roach's cabbage-patch.
Potatoes, lettuce, cabbage, peas
Could all be had with perfect ease
(Provided you had first checked out
That Mister Roach was not about.)
The Tortoise had for very long
Enjoyed this lovely restaurant,
But all at once – Oh, shame! Disgrace!
A ghastly thing was taking place!
That horrid Hare began to poach
The sacred land of Mister Roach.

And worst of all, the Hare got rid
Of far more than the Tortoise did.
With beans he'd eat up every one
Before the Tortoise had begun!
The carrots all were out of sight
Before poor Torty had one bite!
The lettuce, succulent and green,
Was suddenly no longer seen!
And so the Tortoise now began
To hatch a very subtle plan.
He came across the Hare at dawn
Demolishing a row of corn,
And said to him, "Would you agree
To have a sporting bet with me?
I don't believe I've ever met
A hare who could refuse a bet."
Hare said, "I must admit I play
The horses almost every day."
The Tortoise said, "I'm betting you
I'd win a race between us two."

"You're round the twist!" the Hare cried out.
"You're bonkersville! You're up the spout!
Why, I could run to Equador
Before you'd even crossed the floor!
I'd run from here to Cowdenbeath
Before you'd even brushed your teeth!
I'd run to Poole and Beachy Head
Before you're hardly out of bed!
Don't talk to me of how to run!
A hare can outpace anyone!"
The Tortoise said, "Although you're fast
I'm betting you you'll come in last.
And by the way, you might recall
Pride always comes before a fall."
The Hare was so convulsed with scorn
He nearly choked upon his corn.
He gagged and coughed, but when he spake
He cried, "You're on! So what's the stake?"

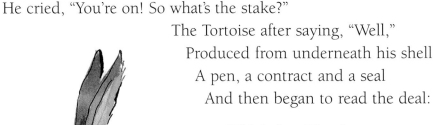

    The Tortoise after saying, "Well,"
      Produced from underneath his shell
      A pen, a contract and a seal
      And then began to read the deal:

        "If I do lose I hereby swear
         That I will nevermore go near
          Or take the tiniest of nibbles
           From Mister Roach's vegitibbles."

        The Hare considered for a while,
        Then answered with a knowing smile,
        "That all seems eminently fair,"
        And signed it with a flourish – *Hare*.

The Hare was later heard to say
Quite loudly, in a scornful way,
"Well Torty, when this race is run,
When you have lost and I have won,
I don't know where you'll go to dine,
But that is no concern of mine."
The Tortoise now went on to call
On Mister Rat at evenfall,
And found him in his workshop where
The Rat was trying to repair
A fascinatingly bizarre
Bright saffron-yellow motor-car.
The Rat was famous everywhere
As being a brilliant engineer,
But just like all the ratty clan
He was a crafty business man
And well-nigh guaranteed to rob
His customers on every job.

"Hello, old Rat," the Tortoise cries,
Regarding him through scaly eyes.
"I've come along tonight to ask
About a highly secret task."
Rat, slowly putting down his spanner,
Assumed a sympathetic manner.
"My dear old Torty," he declared,
"Now if you want your car repaired . . ."
"No, no!" the Tortoise cried. "You're wrong.
Now here's the burden of my song."
He then explained with skill and flair
The details of his bet with Hare.
The Rat said, "Ho! I do believe
There's something fishy up your sleeve.
It's obvious if the race was fair
You'd have no chance against the Hare.
In fact, however much you cheat,
You'll never never never beat
That speedy Hare. You are a dope
To think you have the slightest hope."

The Tortoise said, "There is, old Rat,
More ways than one to skin a cat."
Rat cried, "Be sensible, old man!
Look, even if I were to ram
A red-hot poker up your blaster,
You wouldn't travel any faster."
"Hold it!" the Tortoise cried. "My wheeze,
And listen carefully if you please,
My brilliant wonderful idea
Is that you build for me right here
A little four-wheeled motor-car
That travels fast and very far,
Which you can screw beneath my shell
In such a way no man can tell,
Not even bright-eyed Mister Hare,
That I've got anything down there.
I'll wave my legs and off I'll go
And Mister Hare will never know
What's giving me this wondrous power
To run at sixty miles an hour.
Oh Rat, I know you'll do it right –
The little wheels just out of sight,
The engine tucked away as well,
All hidden underneath my shell!"
The Rat was stunned. He stretched his eyes,
He stood and shouted with surprise,
"By gum, I never would have guessed
An ancient bird like you possessed
Such genius in your upper storey!
This has to be your path to glory!
I'll do the job this very night
Provided that the price is right."

"How much? How much?" the Tortoise cried.
"That all depends," the Rat replied,
"Which motor you require on board,
A Rolls, a Bentley or a Ford?"
"The fastest one!" the Tortoise said.
"I want a racing thoroughbred!"
The deal was struck, arrangements made
And willingly the Tortoise paid.
As soon as Rat was all alone
He tiptoed to the telephone
And asked to speak to Mister Hare,
And said, "Hello, it's Ratty here."
The Hare said, "Hello Rat, what's new?
And how are things tonight with you?"
Rat answered, "Would you pay a lot
To hear about an evil plot?
    Would you, for instance, give your shirt
        To know who's going to do you dirt?"
            There was a silence on the line,
                Then Hare cried, "Who's the rotten swine?
                Come on now, Ratty, tell me true!
                You know I'd do the same for you!"
                The Rat said, very soft and sly,
                "No go, old man. Goodbye, goodbye."
                "Wait! Wait!" cried Hare. "Don't go away!
                How much d'you want? I'll pay! I'll pay!"
                And so once more old Ratty made
                A very advantageous trade,
                And after he had got his fee
                He told of Torty's villainy.
                The Hare jumped up and down and cried,
                "That's cheating! He's disqualified!"

The Rat, with nauseating joy,
Said, "Hate to tell you this, old boy,
Your contract simply says you race,
The two of you, from place to place.
It doesn't ban the clever use
Of engines giving extra juice."
"I'm cooked!' the Hare yelled out. "I'm done!
I'll lose my favourite restaurant!'
The Rat said, slimier than ever,
"Are you forgetting rats are clever?
I'm sure arrangements could be made
Provided *extra* cash is paid.
I could for instance guarantee,
In token of this extra fee,
That irrespective of how fast
The Tortoise goes, you won't be last.
I'd see that all his tyres go flat,
I'd guarantee it," said the Rat.

    "How much, how much?" the other cried.
    "An awful lot," the Rat replied.
      The Hare now paid a second bill,
        Dirty Rat got richer still.

      This thrilling epoch-making race
        Was by agreement taking place
          Along the road beneath the hill
            To finish by the barley-mill.
              The Rat meanwhile had tipped a load
              Of spiky nails across the road,
              Then hid himself, when that was done,
              Behind the hedge to see the fun.

Spectators all along the way
Had come to watch and shout hooray,
The field-mice, weasels, hedgehogs, stoats
And rabbits in their furry coats
All lined the route and waved their flags
And picnicked out of paper-bags.
An ancient fox who ran the show
Yelled out, "Get ready! Steady! Go!"

Now Torty gunned his great machine
And off he went in clouds of steam,
And soon because of all that power
Was doing fifty miles an hour.
Each time he had to change a gear,
Black smoke came belching from his rear.
Each time he had to use the brake,
His shell began to creak and shake.
But oh, it was a wondrous thing
To see a tortoise on the wing.
"I'm going to win with lengths to spare!"
The Tortoise yelled to Mister Hare.
"Oh no you're not!" the Hare replied,
"For I've got Ratty on my side!"
And just a moment after that
All four of Torty's tyres went flat.

He had to stop. He had no choice,
And Hare, in an exultant voice,
Cried out, "Well, that's the end of you!
Stand back! Stand back! I'm coming through!"
The Hare forgot that just ahead
Lay all the nails that Rat had spread.
The spiky things were everywhere
And silly foolish Mister Hare
Had spikes in every foot and toe!
He couldn't run! He couldn't go!
He shouted, "I can run no more!
We'll have to call the race a draw."
The Tortoise, all his tyres flat,
Said sadly, "I agree to that."

Meanwhile the dirty Mister Rat
Went home and counted all his pay.
He'd had a profitable day.
So just remember if you can,
Don't tangle with a business man.
It doesn't matter who you choose,
They always win, we always lose.
If you were here and I was there,
If you were Tortoise, I was Hare,
We'd both get diddled in the end
By people like our Ratty friend.

The Shark

Previously unpublished
Illustrated by Lane Smith

Deep down within the waters dark
There lurks the dangerous Mister Shark.
He waits there hoping he will meet
Something delicious he can eat.
His teeth are sharp and very long
And so exceptionally strong
That often (simply out of spite)
With one enormous powerful bite
He'll take a fully grown giraffe
And cut the creature clean in half.
"Oh, Mister Shark, you dirty beast,
Is poor giraffe your favourite feast?"
"Oh, not by any means," he'll say,
The dish he dreams about all day
For breakfast dinner lunch and tea,
His favourite food is . . . you and me.

He likes us big, he likes us small,
He likes to eat us clothes and all.

"So darling Jim, I beg, I pray,
Remember what I'm going to say;
Do not go bathing in the sea
Along this coast where sharks might be.
When you're with us, the golden rule
Is always use the swimming-pool . . .
Are you quite sure you heard me, dear?
Good gracious me, the boy's not here!
Jimmy, Jim, Jim! Where are you, Jim?
Oh gosh, I'll bet he's gone to swim!"

The woman ran flat-out to reach
The lovely glistening sandy beach.
The sea was calm and still and green
But Jim was nowhere to be seen.

Deep down within the waters dark
There lurked the dangerous Mister Shark.
He lay there gnawing, nibbling, munching,
Chewing, burping, grinning, crunching,
Until the whole of little Jim
Was pretty much inside of him.
He murmured as he ate the feet,
"Small boys are awfully good to eat."

Part Three

UNLIKELY
CREATURES

The Grobes

from CHARLIE AND THE GREAT GLASS ELEVATOR
Illustrated by Chris Wormell

In the quelchy quaggy sogmire,
In the mashy mideous harshland,
At the witchy hour of gloomness,
All the grobes come oozing home.

You can hear them softly slimeing,
Glissing hissing o'er the slubber,
All those oily boily bodies
Oozing onward in the gloam.

So start to run! Oh, skid and daddle
Through the slubber slush and sossel!
Skip jump hop and try to skaddle!
All the grobes are on the roam!

The Ant-Eater

from DIRTY BEASTS
Illustrated by William Joyce

Some wealthy folks from U.S.A.,
Who lived near San Francisco Bay,
Possessed an only child called Roy,
A plump and unattractive boy –
Half-baked, half-witted and half-boiled,
But worst of all, most dreadfully spoiled.
Whatever Roy desired each day,
His father bought him right away –
Toy motor-cars, electric trains,
The latest model aeroplanes,
A colour television-set,
A saxophone, a clarinet,

Expensive teddy-bears that talked,
And animals that walked and squawked.
That house contained sufficient toys
To thrill a half a million boys.
(As well as this, young Roy would choose,
Two pairs a week of brand-new shoes.)
And now he stood there shouting, "What
On earth is there I haven't got?
How hard to think of something new!
The choices are extremely few!"
Then added, as he scratched his ear,
"Hold it! I've got a good idea!
I think the next thing I must get
Should be a most peculiar pet –
The kind that no one else has got –
A giant ANT-EATER! Why not?"

As soon as father heard the news,
He quickly wrote to all the zoos.
"Sirs," he said, "My dear keepers,
Do any of you have ant-eaters?"
They answered all by return of mail.
"Our ant-eaters are not for sale."
Undaunted, Roy's fond parent hurled
More messages across the world.
He said, "I'll pay you through the nose
If you can get me one of those."
At last he found an Indian gent
(He lived near Delhi, in a tent),
Who said that he would sacrifice
His pet for an enormous price
(The price demanded, if you please,
Was fifty thousand gold rupees).
The ant-eater arrived half-dead.
It looked at Roy and softly said,
"I'm famished. Do you think you could
Please give me just a little food?
A crust of bread, a bit of meat?
I haven't had a thing to eat
In all the time I was at sea,
For nobody looked after me."
Roy shouted, "No! No bread or meat!
Go find some ants! They're what you eat!"
The starving creature crawled away.
It searched the garden night and day,
It hunted every inch of ground,
But not one single ant it found.
"Please give me food!" the creature cried.

"Go find an ant!" the boy replied.
By chance, upon that very day,
Roy's father's sister came to stay –
A foul old hag of eighty-three
Whose name, it seems, was Dorothy.
She said to Roy, "Come let us sit
Out in the sun and talk a bit."
Roy said, "I don't believe you've met
My new and most unusual pet?"
He pointed down among the stones
Where something lay, all skin and bones.
"Ant-eater!" he yelled. "Don't lie there yawning!
This is my ant! Come say good-morning!"
(Some people in the U.S.A.
Have trouble with the words they say.
However hard they try, they can't
Pronounce a simple word like AUNT.
Instead of AUNT, they call it ANT,
Instead of CAN'T, they call it KANT.)
Roy yelled, "Come here, you so-and-so!
My ant would like to say hello!"
Slowly, the creature raised its head.
"D'you mean that that's an *ant*?" it said.
"Of course!" cried Roy. "Ant Dorothy!
This ant is over eighty-three."
The creature smiled. Its tummy rumbled.
It licked its starving lips and mumbled,
"A giant ant! By gosh, a winner!
At last I'll get a decent dinner!
No matter if it's eighty-three.
If that's an ant, then it's for me!"

Then, taking very careful aim,
It pounced upon the startled dame.
It grabbed her firmly by the hair
And ate her up right then and there,
Murmuring as it chewed the feet,
"The largest ant I'll ever eat."
Meanwhile, our hero Roy had sped
In terror to the potting-shed,
And tried to make himself obscure
Behind a pile of horse-manure.
But ant-eater came sneaking in
(Already it was much less thin)
And said to Roy, "You little squirt,
I think I'll have you for dessert."

The Tummy Beast

from DIRTY BEASTS
Illustrated by Babette Cole

One afternoon I said to mummy,
"Who is this person in my tummy?
He must be small and very thin
Or how could he have gotten in?"
My mother said from where she sat,
"It isn't nice to talk like that."
"It's true!" I cried. "I swear it, mummy!
There *is* a person in my tummy!
He talks to me at night in bed,
He's always asking to be fed,
Throughout the day, he screams at me,
Demanding sugar buns for tea.
He tells me it is not a sin
To go and raid the biscuit tin.
I know quite well it's awfully wrong
To guzzle food the whole day long,
But really I can't help it, mummy,
Not with this person in my tummy."
"You horrid child!" my mother cried.
"Admit it right away, you've lied!
You're simply trying to produce
A silly asinine excuse!
You are the greedy guzzling brat!
And that is why you're always fat!"
I tried once more, "*Believe me*, mummy,
There *is* a person in my tummy."

"I've had enough!" my mother said,
"You'd better go at once to bed!"
Just then, a nicely timed event
Delivered me from punishment.
Deep in my tummy something stirred,
And then an awful noise was heard,
A snorting grumbling grunting sound
That made my tummy jump around.
My darling mother nearly died,
"My goodness, what was that?" she cried.
At once, the tummy voice came through,
It shouted, "Hey there! Listen you!
I'm getting hungry! I want eats!
I want lots of chocs and sweets!
Get me half a pound of nuts!
Look snappy or I'll twist your guts!"
"That's him!" I cried. *"He's in my tummy!*
So now do you believe me, mummy?"

But mummy answered nothing more,
For she had fainted on the floor.

The Toad and the Snail

from DIRTY BEASTS
Illustrated by Chris Wormell

I really am most awfully fond
Of playing in the lily-pond.
I take off shoes and socks and coat
And paddle with my little boat.
Now yesterday, quite suddenly,
A giant toad came up to me.
This toad was easily as big
As any fair-sized fattish pig.
He smiled and said, "How do you do?
Hello! Good morning! How are you?"
(His face somehow reminded me
Of mummy's sister Emily.)

The toad said, "Don't you think I'm fine?
Admire these lovely legs of mine,
And I am sure you've never seen
A toad so gloriously green!"
I said, "So far as I can see,
You look just like Aunt Emily."
He said, "I'll bet Aunt Emily
Can't jump one half as high as me.
Hop on my back, young friend," he cried,
"I'll take you for a marvellous ride."
As I got on, I thought, oh blimey,
Oh, deary me, how wet and slimy!
"Sit further back," he said. "That's right.
I'm going to jump, so hold on tight."
He jumped! Oh, how he jumped! By gum,
I thought my final hour had come!
My wretched eardrums popped and fizzed.
My eyeballs watered. Up we whizzed.
I clung on tight. I shouted, "How
Much further are we going now?"
Toad said, his face all wreathed in smiles,
"With every jump, it's fifty miles!"
Quite literally, we jumped all over,
From Scotland to the Cliffs of Dover!
Above the Cliffs, we stopped for tea,
And Toad said, gazing at the sea,
"What do you say we take a chance,
And jump from England into France?"
I said, "Oh dear, d'you think we oughta?
I'd hate to finish in the water."
But toads, you'll find, don't give a wink
For what we little children think.

He didn't bother to reply.
He jumped! You should have seen us fly!
We simply soared across the sea,
The marvellous Mister Toad and me.

Then down we came, and down and down,
And landed in a funny town.
We landed hard, in fact we bounced.
"We're there! It's France!" the Toad announced.
He said, "You must admit it's grand
To jump into a foreign land.
No boats, no bicycles, no trains,
No cars, no noisy aeroplanes."
Just then, we heard a fearful shout,
"Oh, heavens above!" the Toad cried out.
I turned and saw a frightening sight –
On every side, to left, to right,
People were running down the road,
Running at me and Mister Toad,
And every person, man and wife
Was brandishing a carving-knife.
It didn't take me very long
To figure there was something wrong.
And yet, how could a small boy know,
For nobody had told me so,
That Frenchmen aren't like you or me,
They do things very differently.
They won't say "yards", they call them "metres",
And they're the *most peculiar* eaters:
A Frenchman frequently regales
Himself with half-a-dozen SNAILS!
The greedy ones will gulp a score
Of these foul brutes and ask for more.
(In many of the best hotels
The people also eat the shells.)
Imagine that! My stomach turns!
One might as well eat slugs or worms!
But wait. Read on a little bit.
You haven't heard the half of it.

These French go even more agog
If someone offers them a FROG!
(You'd better fetch a basin quick
In case you're going to be sick.)
The bits of frog they like to eat
Are thighs and calves and toes and feet.
The French will gobble loads and loads
Of legs they chop off frogs and toads.
They think it's absolutely ripping
To guzzle frogs-legs fried in dripping.
That's why the whole town and their wives
Were rushing us with carving-knives.
They screamed in French, "Well I'll be blowed!
What legs there are upon that toad!
Chop them! Skin them! Cook them! Fry them!
All of us are going to try them!"
"Toad!" I cried. "I'm not a funk,
But ought we not to do a bunk?
These rascals haven't come to greet you.
All they want to do is eat you!"
Toad turned his head and looked at me,
And said, as cool as cool could be,
"Calm down and listen carefully please,
I often come to France to tease
These crazy French who long to eat
My lovely tender froggy meat.
I am a MAGIC TOAD!" he cried.
"And I don't ever have to hide!
Stay where you are! Don't move!" he said,
And pressed a button on his head.
At once, there came a blinding flash,
And then the most almighty crash,
And sparks were bursting all around,
And smoke was rising from the ground . . .

When all the smoke had cleared away
The Frenchmen with their knives cried, "*Hey!*
Where is the toad? Where has he gone?"
You see, I now was sitting on
A wonderfully ENORMOUS SNAIL!
His shell was smooth and brown and pale,
And I was so high off the ground
That I could see for miles around.
The Snail said, "Hello! Greetings! Hail!
I was a Toad. Now I'm a Snail.
I had to change the way I looked
To save myself from being cooked."
"Oh Snail," I said, "I'm not so sure.
I think they're starting up once more."
The French were shouting, "What a snail!
Oh, what a monster! What a whale!
He makes the toad look titchy small!
There's lovely snail-meat for us all!

We'll bake the creature in his shell
And ring aloud the dinner-bell!
Get garlic, parsley, butter, spices!
We'll cut him into fifty slices!
Come sharpen up your carving-knives!
This is the banquet of our lives!"
I murmured through my quivering lips,
"Oh Snail, I think we've had our chips."
The Snail replied, "I disagree.
Those greedy French, they'll not eat me."
But on they came. They screamed, "Yahoo!
Surround the brute and run him through!"
Good gracious, I could almost feel
The pointed blades, the shining steel!
But Snail was cool as cool could be.
He turned his head and winked at me,
And murmured, "Au revoir, farewell,"
And pulled a lever on his shell.

I looked around. The Snail had gone!
And *now* who was I sitting on? . . .
Oh what relief! What joy! Because
At last I'd found a friend. It was
The gorgeous, glamorous, absurd,
Enchanting ROLY-POLY BIRD!
He turned and whispered in my ear,
"Well, fancy seeing you, my dear!"
Then up he went in glorious flight.
I clutched his neck and hung on tight.
We fairly raced across the sky,
The Roly-Poly Bird and I,
And landed safely just beyond
The fringes of the lily-pond.

When I got home I never told
A solitary single soul
What I had done or where I'd been
Or any of the things I'd seen.
I did not even say I rode
Upon a giant jumping toad,
'Cause if I had, I knew that they
Would not believe me anyway.
But you and I know well it's true.
We know I jumped, we know I flew.
We're sure it all took place, although
Not one of us will ever know,
We'll never, never understand
Why children go to Wonderland.

The Porcupine

from DIRTY BEASTS

Illustrated by Satoshi Kitamura

Each Saturday I shout "Hooray!"
For that's my pocket-money day,
(Although it's clearly understood
I only get it when I'm good.)
This week my parents had been told
That I had been as good as gold,
So after breakfast 50p
My generous father gave to me.
Like lightning down the road I ran
Until I reached the sweet-shop man,
And bought the chocolates of my dreams,
A great big bag of raspberry creams.

There is a secret place I know
Where I quite often like to go,
Beyond the wood, behind some rocks,
A super place for guzzling chocs.
When I arrived, I quickly found
A comfy-looking little mound,
Quite clean and round and earthy-brown –
Just right, I thought, for sitting down.
Here I will sit all morning long
And eat until my chocs are gone.
I sat. I screamed. I jumped a foot!
Would you believe that I had put
That tender little rump of mine
Upon a giant porcupine!
My backside seemed to catch on fire!
A hundred red-hot bits of wire
A hundred prickles sticking in
And puncturing my precious skin!

I ran for home. I shouted, "Mum!
Behold the prickles in my bum!"
My mum, who always keeps her head,
Bent down to look and then she said,
"I personally am not about
To try to pull *those* prickles out.
I think a job like this requires
The services of Mr Myers."
I shouted, "Not the dentist! No!
Oh mum, why don't *you* have a go?"
I begged her twice, I begged her thrice,
But grown-ups never take advice.
She said, "A dentist's very strong.
He pulls things out the whole day long."
She drove me quickly into town,
And then they turned me upside-down
Upon the awful dentist's chair,
While two strong nurses held me there.

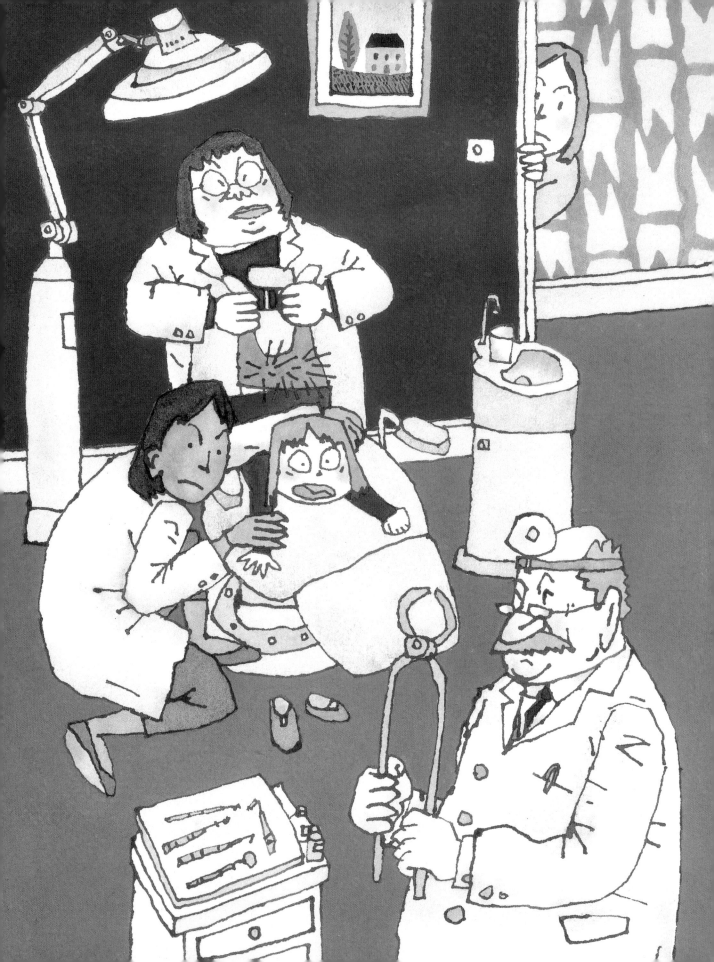

Enter the dreaded Mr Myers
Waving a massive pair of pliers.
"This is," he cried with obvious glee,
"A new experience for me.
Quite honestly I can't pretend
I've ever pulled things from *this* end."
He started pulling one by one
And yelling "My, oh my, what fun!"
I shouted "Help!" I shouted "Ow!"
He said, "It's nearly over now.
For heaven's sake, don't squirm about!
Here goes! The last one's coming out!"
The dentist pulled and out it came,
And then I heard the man exclaim,
"Let us now talk about the fees.
That will be fifty guineas, please."
My mother is a gutsy bird
And never one to mince a word.
She cried, "By gosh, that's jolly steep!"
He answered, "No, it's very cheap.
My dear woman, can't you see
That if it hadn't been for me
This child could go another year
With prickles sticking in her rear."

So that was that. Oh, what a day!
And what a fuss! But by the way,
I think I know why porcupines
Surround themselves with prickly spines.
It is to stop some silly clown
From squashing them by sitting down.
Don't copy me. Don't be a twit.
Be sure you LOOK before you SIT.

There's No Knowing
What We Shall See

from JAMES AND THE GIANT PEACH

Illustrated by Emma Chichester Clark

We may see a Creature with forty-nine heads
Who lives in the desolate snow,
And whenever he catches a cold (which he dreads)
He has forty-nine noses to blow.

We may see the venomous Pink-Spotted Scrunch
Who can chew up a man with one bite.
It likes to eat five of them roasted for lunch
And eighteen for its supper at night.

We may see a Dragon, and nobody knows
That we won't see a Unicorn there.
We may see a terrible Monster with toes
Growing out of the tufts of his hair.

We may see the sweet little Biddy-Bright Hen
So playful, so kind and well-bred;
And such beautiful eggs! You just boil them and then
They explode and they blow off your head.

A Gnu and a Gnocerous surely you'll see
And that gnormous and gnorrible Gnat
Whose sting when it stings you goes in at the knee
And comes out through the top of your hat.

We may even get lost and be frozen by frost.
We may die in an earthquake or tremor.
Or nastier still, we may even be tossed
On the horns of a furious Dilemma.

The Nicest Creatures in the World

from JAMES AND THE GIANT PEACH
Illustrated by Alexis Deacon

"My friends, this is the Centipede, and let me make it known
He is so sweet and gentle that (although he's overgrown)
The Queen of Spain, again and again, has summoned him by phone
To baby-sit and sing and knit and be a chaperone
When nurse is off and all the royal children are alone."
("Small wonder," said a Fireman, "they're no longer on the throne.")

"The Earthworm, on the other hand,"
Said James, beginning to expand,
"Is great for digging up the land
And making old soils newer.
Moreover, you should understand
He would be absolutely grand
For digging subway tunnels and
For making you a sewer."
(The Earthworm blushed and beamed with pride.
Miss Spider clapped and cheered and cried,
"Could any words be truer?")

"And the Grasshopper, ladies and gents, is a boon
In millions and millions of ways.
You have only to ask him to give you a tune
And he plays and he plays and he plays.
As a toy for your children he's perfectly sweet;
There's nothing so good in the shops –
You've only to tickle the soles of his feet
And he hops and he hops and he hops."
("He can't be very fierce!" exclaimed
The Head of all the Cops.)

"And now without excuse
I'd like to introduce
This charming Glow-worm, lover of simplicity.
She is easy to install
On your ceiling or your wall,
And although this smacks a bit of eccentricity,
It's really rather clever
For thereafter you will never
You will NEVER NEVER NEVER
Have the slightest need for using electricity."
(At which, no less than fifty-two
Policemen cried, "If this is true
That creature'll get some fabulous publicity!")

"And here we have Miss Spider
With a mile of thread inside her
Who has personally requested me to say
That she's NEVER met Miss Muffet
On her charming little tuffet –
If she had she'd NOT have frightened her away.
Should her looks sometimes alarm you
Then I don't think it would harm you
To repeat at least a hundred times a day:
'I must NEVER kill a spider
I must only help and guide her
And invite her in the nursery to play.'"
(The Police all nodded slightly,
And the Firemen smiled politely,
And about a dozen people cried, "Hooray!")

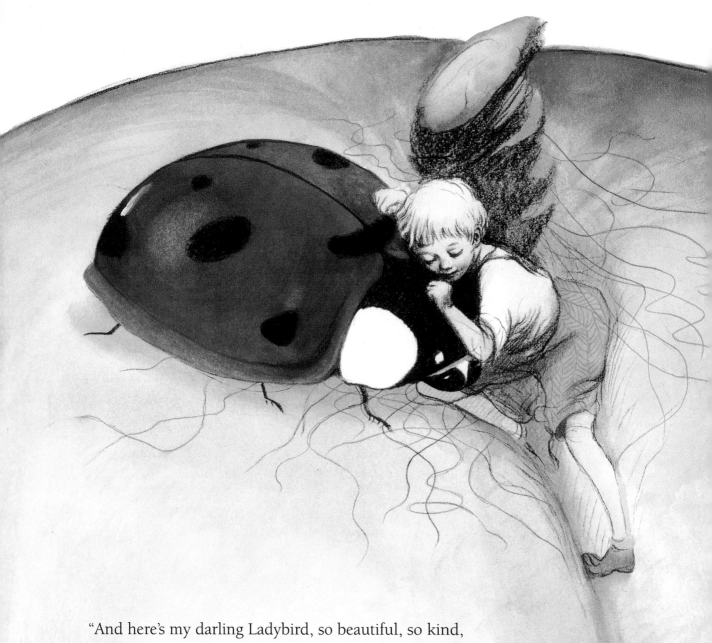

"And here's my darling Ladybird, so beautiful, so kind,
My greatest comfort since this trip began.
She has four hundred children and she's left them all behind,
But they're coming on the next peach if they can."
(The Cops cried, "She's entrancing!"
All the Firemen started dancing,
And the crowds all started cheering to a man!)

"And now, the Silkworm," James went on,
"Whose silk will bear comparison
With all the greatest silks there are
In Rome and Philadelphia.
If you would search the whole world through
From Paraguay to Timbuctoo
I don't think you would find one bit
Of silk that could compare with it.
Even the shops in Singapore
Don't have the stuff. And what is more,
This Silkworm had, I'll have you know,
The honour, not so long ago,
To spin and weave and sew and press
The Queen of England's wedding dress.
And she's already made and sent
A waistcoat for your President."
("Well, good for her!" the Cops cried out,
And all at once a mighty shout
Went up around the Empire State,
"Let's get them down at once! Why WAIT?")

Willy Wonka's Song of Defiance to the Knids

from CHARLIE AND THE GREAT GLASS ELEVATOR
Illustrated by Joann Sfar

"Oh you Knid, you are vile and vermicious!"
cried Mr Wonka.

"You are slimy and soggy and squishous!
But what do we care
'Cause you can't get in here,
So hop it and don't get ambitious!"

Later he taunts them again . . .

"Hello, you great Knid! Tell us, how do you do?
You're a rather strange colour today.
Your bottom is purple and lavender blue.
Should it really be looking that way?

"Are you not feeling well? Are you going to faint?
Is it something we cannot discuss?
It must be a very unpleasant complaint,
For your backside's as big as a bus!

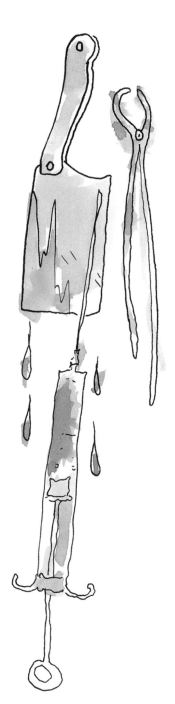

"Let me get you a doctor. I know just the man
For a Knid with a nasty disease.
He's a butcher by trade which is not a bad plan,
And he charges quite reasonable fees.

"Ah, here he is now! 'Doc, you really are kind
To travel so far into space.
There's your patient, the Knid with the purple behind!
Do you think it's a desperate case?'

"'Great heavens above! It's no wonder he's pale!'
Said the doc with a horrible grin.
'There's a sort of balloon on the end of his tail!
I must prick it at once with a pin!'

"So he got out a thing like an Indian spear,
With feathers all over the top,
And he lunged and he caught the Knid smack
  in the rear,
But alas, the balloon didn't pop!

"Cried the Knid, 'What on earth am I going to do
With this painful preposterous lump?
I can't remain standing the whole summer through!
And I cannot sit down on my rump!'

"'It's a bad case of rear-ache,' the medico said,
'And it's something I cannot repair.
If you want to sit down, you must sit on your head,
With your bottom high up in the air!'"

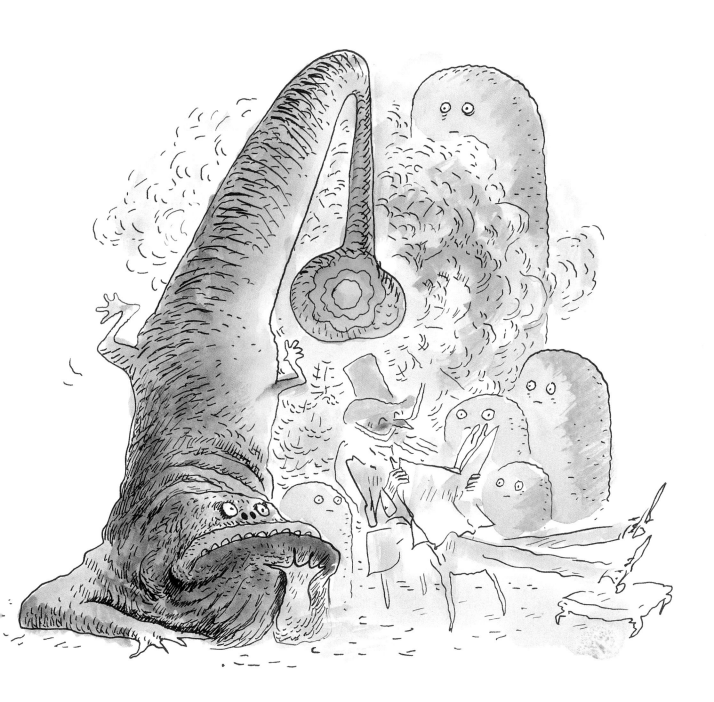

Part Four

POISONOUS POSSIBILITIES

Down Vith Children!

from THE WITCHES
Illustrated by Bee Willey

Down vith children! Do them in!
Boil their bones and fry their skin!
Bish them, sqvish them, bash them, mash them!
Brrreak them, shake them, slash them, smash them!
Offer chocs vith magic powder!
Say "Eat up!" then say it louder.
Crrram them full of sticky eats,
Send them home still guzzling sveets.
And in the morning little fools
Go marching off to separate schools.
A girl feels sick and goes all pale.
She yells, "Hey look! I've grrrown a tail!"
A boy who's standing next to her
Screams, "Help! I think I'm grrrowing fur!"
Another shouts, "Vee look like frrreaks!
There's viskers growing on our cheeks!"
A boy who vos extremely tall
Cries out, "Vot's wrong? I'm grrrowing small!"
Four tiny legs begin to sprrrout
From everybody rrround about.
And all at vunce, all in a trrrice,
There are no children! Only MICE!
In every school is mice galore
All rrrunning rrround the school-rrroom floor!
And all the poor demented teachers
Is yelling, "Hey, who are these crrreatures?"
They stand upon the desks and shout,
"Get out, you filthy mice! Get out!
Vill someone fetch some mouse-trrraps, please!
And don't forrrget to bring the cheese!"

Now mouse-trrraps come and every trrrap
Goes *snippy-snip* and *snappy-snap*.
The mouse-trrraps have a powerful spring,
The springs go *crack* and *snap* and *ping!*
Is lovely noise for us to hear!
Is music to a vitch's ear!
Dead mice is every place arrround,
Piled two feet deep upon the grrround,
Vith teachers searching left and rrright,
But not a single child in sight!
The teachers cry, "Vot's going on?
Oh vhere have all the children gone?
Is half-past nine and as a rrrule
They're never late as this for school!"
Poor teachers don't know vot to do.
Some sit and rrread, and just a few
Amuse themselves throughout the day
By sweeping all the mice avay.
AND ALL US VITCHES SHOUT HOORAY!

George's Marvellous Medicine

from GEORGE'S MARVELLOUS MEDICINE
Illustrated by Neal Layton

"So give me a bug and a jumping flea,
Give me two snails and lizards three,
And a slimy squiggler from the sea,
And the poisonous sting of a bumblebee,
And the juice from the fruit of the ju-jube tree,
And the powdered bone of a wombat's knee.
And one hundred other things as well
Each with a rather nasty smell.
I'll stir them up, I'll boil them long,
A mixture tough, a mixture strong.

"And then, heigh-ho, and down it goes,
A nice big spoonful (hold your nose)
Just gulp it down and have no fear.
"How do you like it, Granny dear?"
Will she go pop? Will she explode?
Will she go flying down the road?
Will she go poof in a puff of smoke?
Start fizzing like a can of Coke?
Who knows? Not I. Let's wait and see.
(I'm glad it's neither you nor me.)
Oh Grandma, if you only knew
What I have got in store for you!

"Fiery broth and witch's brew
Foamy froth and riches blue
Fume and spume and spoondrift spray
Fizzle swizzle shout hooray
Watch it sloshing, swashing, sploshing
Hear it hissing, squishing, spissing
Grandma better start to pray."

(The following verses were included in the U.S. edition of the book.)

"Here we go then," cried George, jumping up from the table . . .

"A magic medicine it shall be!
A marvellous mixture bright!
I think that I can guarantee
To give the hag a fright,
But we shall have to wait and see
If I can get it right.

"I'll mix some pretty funny things
Together in the pot,
Like hornets' stings and dragons' wings,
And then I'll add a lot
Of goblins' gunge and fairy rings
And anything I've got.

"Will she go bang? Will she go squish?
Perhaps she'll disappear.
Maybe she'll steam like new-boiled fish
Or froth like bottled beer.
I'm certain that she'll wish and wish
She'd never had me near.

"Oh Grandma, if you only knew
What I have got in store for you."

I'm Going Going Going

Unpublished verse from GEORGE'S MARVELLOUS MEDICINE
Illustrated by Neal Layton

Oh, I'm going going going!
Oh, I'm growing growing growing!
I can feel that medicine flowing!
Oh, it's burning and it's glowing!
There's no earthly way of knowing
Just how long I'll go on growing!
Give me another dose, my boy,
And let's go through the roof!
Your marvellous medicine's magic joy,
And I'm the living proof!

Goldie Pinklesweet

from CHARLIE AND THE GREAT GLASS ELEVATOR
Illustrated by Tony Ross

Did any of you ever meet
A child called Goldie Pinklesweet?
Who on her seventh birthday went
To stay with Granny down in Kent.
At lunchtime on the second day
Of dearest little Goldie's stay,

Granny announced, "I'm going down
To do some shopping in the town."
(D'you know why Granny didn't tell
The child to come along as well?
She's going to the nearest inn
To buy herself a double gin.)

So out she creeps. She shuts the door.
And Goldie, after making sure
That she is really by herself,
Goes quickly to the medicine shelf,
And there, her little greedy eyes
See pills of every shape and size,
Such fascinating colours too –
Some green, some pink, some brown, some blue.
"All right," she says, "let's try the brown."
She takes one pill and gulps it down.
"Yum-yum!" she cries. "Hooray! What fun!
They're chocolate-coated, every one!"
She gobbles five, she gobbles ten,
She stops her gobbling only when
The last pill's gone. There are no more.
Slowly she rises from the floor.
She stops. She hiccups. Dear, oh dear,
She starts to feel a trifle queer.

You see, how could young Goldie know,
For nobody had told her so,
That Grandmama, her old relation,
Suffered from frightful constipation.
This meant that every night she'd give
Herself a powerful laxative,
And all the medicines that she'd bought
Were naturally of this sort.
The pink and red and blue and green
Were all extremely strong and mean.
But far more fierce and meaner still,
Was Granny's little chocolate pill.
Its blast effect was quite uncanny.
It used to shake up even Granny.
In point of fact she did not dare
To use them more than twice a year.
So can you wonder little Goldie
Began to feel a wee bit mouldy?

Inside her tummy, something stirred.
A funny gurgling sound was heard,
And then, oh dear, from deep within,
The ghastly rumbling sounds begin!
They rumbilate and roar and boom!
They bounce and echo round the room!
The floorboards shake and from the wall
Some bits of paint and plaster fall.
Explosions, whistles, awful bangs
Were followed by the loudest clangs.
(A man next door was heard to say,
"A thunderstorm is on the way.")
But on and on the rumbling goes.
A window cracks, a lamp-bulb blows.

Young Goldie clutched herself and cried,
"There's something wrong with my inside!"
This was, we very greatly fear,
The understatement of the year.
For wouldn't any child feel crummy,
With loud explosions in her tummy?

Granny, at half past two, came in,
Weaving a little from the gin,
But even so she quickly saw
The empty bottle on the floor.
"My precious laxatives!" she cried.
"I don't feel well," the girl replied.

Angrily Grandma shook her head.
"I'm really not surprised," she said.
"Why can't you leave my pills alone?"
With that, she grabbed the telephone
And shouted, "Listen, send us quick
An ambulance! A child is sick!
It's number fifty, Fontwell Road!
Come fast! I think she might explode!"

We're sure you do not wish to hear
About the hospital and where
They did a lot of horrid things
With stomach-pumps and rubber rings.
Let's answer what you want to know:
Did Goldie live or did she go?
The doctors gathered round her bed.
"There's really not much hope," they said.
"She's going, going, gone!" they cried.
"She's had her chips! She's dead! She's dead!"
"I'm not so sure," the child replied.
And all at once she opened wide
Her great big bluish eyes and sighed,
And gave the anxious docs a wink,
And said, "I'll be okay, I think."

So Goldie lived and back she went
At first to Granny's place in Kent.
Her father came the second day
And fetched her in a Chevrolet,
And drove her to their home in Dover.
But Goldie's troubles were not over.
You see, if someone takes enough
Of any highly dangerous stuff,
One will invariably find
Some traces of it left behind.
It pains us greatly to relate
That Goldie suffered from this fate.
She'd taken such a massive fill
Of this unpleasant kind of pill,
It got into her blood and bones,
It messed up all her chromosomes,
It made her constantly upset,
And she could never really get
The beastly stuff to go away.

And so the girl was forced to stay
For seven hours every day
Within the everlasting gloom
Of what we call the Ladies Room.
And after all, the W.C.
Is not the gayest place to be.
So now, before it is too late,
Take heed of Goldie's dreadful fate.
And seriously, all jokes apart,
Do promise us across your heart
That you will never help yourself
To medicine from the medicine shelf.

137

Part Five

LOOK WHO'S HERE

Aunt Sponge and Aunt Spiker About Themselves

from JAMES AND THE GIANT PEACH

Illustrated by Babette Cole

"I look and smell," Aunt Sponge declared, "as lovely as a rose!
Just feast your eyes upon my face, observe my shapely nose!
Behold my heavenly silky locks!
And if I take off both my socks
You'll see my dainty toes."
"But don't forget," Aunt Spiker cried, "how much your tummy shows!"

Aunt Sponge went red. Aunt Spiker said, "My sweet, you cannot win,
Behold MY gorgeous curvy shape, my teeth, my charming grin!
Oh, beauteous me! How I adore
My radiant looks! And please ignore
The pimple on my chin."
"My dear old trout!" Aunt Sponge cried out, "You're only bones and skin!"

"Such loveliness as I possess can only truly shine
In Hollywood!" Aunt Sponge declared. "Oh, wouldn't that be fine!
I'd capture all the nations' hearts!
They'd give me all the leading parts!
The stars would all resign!"
"I think you'd make," Aunt Spiker said, "a lovely Frankenstein."

The Centipede's Song of Aunt Sponge and Aunt Spiker

from JAMES AND THE GIANT PEACH
Illustrated by Babette Cole

"Aunt Sponge was terrifically fat,
And tremendously flabby at that.
Her tummy and waist
Were as soggy as paste –
It was worse on the place where she sat!

So she said, 'I must make myself flat.
I must make myself sleek as a cat.
I shall do without dinner
To make myself thinner.'
But along came the peach!
Oh, the beautiful peach!
And made her far thinner than that!"

"That was very nice," Miss Spider said. "Now sing one about Aunt Spiker."
"With pleasure," the Centipede answered, grinning:

"Aunt Spiker was thin as a wire,
And dry as a bone, only drier.
She was so long and thin
If you carried her in
You could use her for poking the fire!

"'I must do something quickly,' she frowned.
'I want FAT. I want pound upon pound!
I must eat lots and lots
Of marshmallows and chocs
Till I start bulging out all around.'

"'Ah, yes,' she announced, 'I have sworn
That I'll alter my figure by dawn!'
Cried the peach with a snigger,
'I'LL alter your figure—'
And ironed her out on the lawn!"

The Nurse's Song

from CHARLIE AND THE GREAT GLASS ELEVATOR
Illustrated by Chris Riddell

This mighty man of whom I sing,
The greatest of them all,
Was once a teeny little thing,
Just eighteen inches tall.

I knew him as a tiny tot.
I nursed him on my knee.
I used to sit him on the pot
And wait for him to wee.

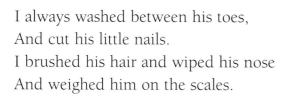

I always washed between his toes,
And cut his little nails.
I brushed his hair and wiped his nose
And weighed him on the scales.

Through happy childhood days he strayed,
    As all nice children should.
I smacked him when he disobeyed,
    And stopped when he was good.

It soon began to dawn on me
    He wasn't very bright,
Because when he was twenty-three
    He couldn't read or write.

"What shall we do?" his parents sobbed.
    "The boy has got the vapours!
He couldn't even get a job
    Delivering the papers!"

"Ah-ha," I said. "This little clot
    Could be a politician."
"Nanny," he cried. "Oh Nanny, what
    A super proposition!"

"Okay," I said. "Let's learn and note
The art of politics.
Let's teach you how to miss the boat
And how to drop some bricks,
And how to win the people's vote
And lots of other tricks.

"Let's learn to make a speech a day
Upon the TV screen,
In which you never never say
Exactly what you mean.

"And most important, by the way,
Is not to let your teeth decay,
And keep your fingers clean."

And now that I am eighty-nine,
It's too late to repent.
The fault was mine the little swine
Became the President.

Jack and Jill

Previously unpublished
Illustrated by Russell Ayto

Jack's mother was a mean old cow,
She never never would allow
Her son to cast his precious pearls
Before the naughty village girls.
One evening, through the window-pane,
Mum spied Jack going up the lane,
And on his arm, dressed fit to kill,
A pretty little girl called Jill.
Mum flew outside and shouted, "Jack!
Come back at once! Come back! Come back!
Why are you going up the hill
With such a wicked girl as Jill?"
Jack answered with a touch of hauteur,
"We're going to fetch a pail of water."
"*A pail of water*," mother cried.
"What lies you tell! Confess you lied!
Inside our mansion we have got
Taps full of water, cold and hot!
Come help yourself, my little lad,
And send that girl away. She's bad!"
Jack answered, "Mum, I'm sprouting wings!
I've untied all those apron-strings!
I want to do as others do!"
Jill smiled and whispered, "Good for you!"

Boggis and Bunce and Bean

from FANTASTIC MR FOX
Illustrated by Helen Oxenbury

Boggis and Bunce and Bean
One fat, one short, one lean.
These horrible crooks
So different in looks
Were nonetheless equally mean.

Miranda Mary Piker

Unpublished verse from CHARLIE AND THE CHOCOLATE FACTORY
Illustrated by Lauren Child

Oh, Miranda Mary Piker,
How could anybody like her,
Such a rude and disobedient little kid,
So we said why don't we fix her
In the Peanut-Brittle Mixer,
Then we're sure to like her better than we did.
Soon this girl who was so vicious
Will have gotten quite delicious
And her parents will have surely understood
That instead of saying, "Miranda,
Oh, the beast we cannot stand her!"
They'll be saying, "Oh, how tasty and how good!"